#1 School Notebook for Academic Success

THE SWEET TASTE OF ACADEMIC SUCCESS
ACANDY PROCESSING TOOLS
NEW LEARNING TECHNOLOGY FOR
PEAK ACADEMIC PERFORMANCE

✔ Academic Calendar
✔ Take Great Class Notes
✔ Active Listening Skills
✔ Write Test Review Notes
✔ Use Association Cues for Instant and Total Recall
✔ Convert Facts into Test Questions
✔ Review for Retention, Recognition, and Recall
✔ Self-Test for Instant and Total Recall
✔ Power Study Snacks

Make the Grade and Achieve the Dream

SM(A)RTGRADES®
Good Grades Become Great Grades and Great Grades Become Grand Dreams
www.smartgrades.com

® All Rights Reserved.
The Great American Notebook Company
More School Smarts for the Same Smart Price
100 School Notebook Designs and Study Tools
www.aplusgrades.com

2010-2011
Academic Year Calendar

July 10
Su	M	Tu	W	Th	F	Sa
				1	2	3
4	5	6	7	8	9	10
11	12	13	14	15	16	17
18	19	20	21	22	23	24
25	26	27	28	29	30	31

August 10
Su	M	Tu	W	Th	F	Sa
1	2	3	4	5	6	7
8	9	10	11	12	13	14
15	16	17	18	19	20	21
22	23	24	25	26	27	28
29	30	31				

September 10
Su	M	Tu	W	Th	F	Sa
			1	2	3	4
5	6	7	8	9	10	11
12	13	14	15	16	17	18
19	20	21	22	23	24	25
26	27	28	29	30		

October 10
Su	M	Tu	W	Th	F	Sa
					1	2
3	4	5	6	7	8	9
10	11	12	13	14	15	16
17	18	19	20	21	22	23
24	25	26	27	28	29	30
31						

November 10
Su	M	Tu	W	Th	F	Sa
	1	2	3	4	5	6
7	8	9	10	11	12	13
14	15	16	17	18	19	20
21	22	23	24	25	26	27
28	29	30				

December 10
Su	M	Tu	W	Th	F	Sa
			1	2	3	4
5	6	7	8	9	10	11
12	13	14	15	16	17	18
19	20	21	22	23	24	25
26	27	28	29	30	31	

January 11
Su	M	Tu	W	Th	F	Sa
						1
2	3	4	5	6	7	8
9	10	11	12	13	14	15
16	17	18	19	20	21	22
23	24	25	26	27	28	29
30	31					

February 11
Su	M	Tu	W	Th	F	Sa
		1	2	3	4	5
6	7	8	9	10	11	12
13	14	15	16	17	18	19
20	21	22	23	24	25	26
27	28					

March 11
Su	M	Tu	W	Th	F	Sa
		1	2	3	4	5
6	7	8	9	10	11	12
13	14	15	16	17	18	19
20	21	22	23	24	25	26
27	28	29	30	31		

April 11
Su	M	Tu	W	Th	F	Sa
					1	2
3	4	5	6	7	8	9
10	11	12	13	14	15	16
17	18	19	20	21	22	23
24	25	26	27	28	29	30

May 11
Su	M	Tu	W	Th	F	Sa
1	2	3	4	5	6	7
8	9	10	11	12	13	14
15	16	17	18	19	20	21
22	23	24	25	26	27	28
29	30	31				

June 11
Su	M	Tu	W	Th	F	Sa
			1	2	3	4
5	6	7	8	9	10	11
12	13	14	15	16	17	18
19	20	21	22	23	24	25
26	27	28	29	30		

July 11
Su	M	Tu	W	Th	F	Sa
					1	2
3	4	5	6	7	8	9
10	11	12	13	14	15	16
17	18	19	20	21	22	23
24	25	26	27	28	29	30
31						

August 11
Su	M	Tu	W	Th	F	Sa
	1	2	3	4	5	6
7	8	9	10	11	12	13
14	15	16	17	18	19	20
21	22	23	24	25	26	27
28	29	30	31			

Notes:

_____

_____

_____

_____

_____

_____

2011-2012
Academic Year Calendar

July 11
Su	M	Tu	W	Th	F	Sa
					1	2
3	4	5	6	7	8	9
10	11	12	13	14	15	16
17	18	19	20	21	22	23
24	25	26	27	28	29	30
31						

August 11
Su	M	Tu	W	Th	F	Sa
	1	2	3	4	5	6
7	8	9	10	11	12	13
14	15	16	17	18	19	20
21	22	23	24	25	26	27
28	29	30	31			

September 11
Su	M	Tu	W	Th	F	Sa
				1	2	3
4	5	6	7	8	9	10
11	12	13	14	15	16	17
18	19	20	21	22	23	24
25	26	27	28	29	30	

October 11
Su	M	Tu	W	Th	F	Sa
						1
2	3	4	5	6	7	8
9	10	11	12	13	14	15
16	17	18	19	20	21	22
23	24	25	26	27	28	29
30	31					

November 11
Su	M	Tu	W	Th	F	Sa
		1	2	3	4	5
6	7	8	9	10	11	12
13	14	15	16	17	18	19
20	21	22	23	24	25	26
27	28	29	30			

December 11
Su	M	Tu	W	Th	F	Sa
				1	2	3
4	5	6	7	8	9	10
11	12	13	14	15	16	17
18	19	20	21	22	23	24
25	26	27	28	29	30	31

January 12
Su	M	Tu	W	Th	F	Sa
1	2	3	4	5	6	7
8	9	10	11	12	13	14
15	16	17	18	19	20	21
22	23	24	25	26	27	28
29	30	31				

February 12
Su	M	Tu	W	Th	F	Sa
			1	2	3	4
5	6	7	8	9	10	11
12	13	14	15	16	17	18
19	20	21	22	23	24	25
26	27	28	29			

March 12
Su	M	Tu	W	Th	F	Sa
				1	2	3
4	5	6	7	8	9	10
11	12	13	14	15	16	17
18	19	20	21	22	23	24
25	26	27	28	29	30	31

April 12
Su	M	Tu	W	Th	F	Sa
1	2	3	4	5	6	7
8	9	10	11	12	13	14
15	16	17	18	19	20	21
22	23	24	25	26	27	28
29	30					

May 12
Su	M	Tu	W	Th	F	Sa
		1	2	3	4	5
6	7	8	9	10	11	12
13	14	15	16	17	18	19
20	21	22	23	24	25	26
27	28	29	30	31		

June 12
Su	M	Tu	W	Th	F	Sa
					1	2
3	4	5	6	7	8	9
10	11	12	13	14	15	16
17	18	19	20	21	22	23
24	25	26	27	28	29	30

July 12
Su	M	Tu	W	Th	F	Sa
1	2	3	4	5	6	7
8	9	10	11	12	13	14
15	16	17	18	19	20	21
22	23	24	25	26	27	28
29	30	31				

August 12
Su	M	Tu	W	Th	F	Sa
			1	2	3	4
5	6	7	8	9	10	11
12	13	14	15	16	17	18
19	20	21	22	23	24	25
26	27	28	29	30	31	

Notes:

_____

_____

_____

_____

_____

_____

He who asks a question may be a fool for five minutes,
but he who never asks a question remains a fool forever.

Tom J. Connelly

My Class Schedule (fixed)
Class:
Teacher:
Day(s):
Time:

My Regular Study Schedule (variable)
Quiet Study Space:
Day(s):
Time:
My Favorite Power Study Snack to Stay Energized and Focused (see list):

My Teacher's Office Hours
Office Address:
Phone #:
E-mail:
Day(s):
Time:

Nine Good Reasons to Visit Your Teacher:
☐ 1. Introduce yourself
☐ 2. Seek clarification of academic material
☐ 3. Ask for approval of your topic and outline
☐ 4. Seek constructive criticism of your rough draft
☐ 5. To complain about an unfair test question
☐ 6. To correct a grading error
☐ 7. You will be absent from class due to a private matter
☐ 8. Ask for a recommendation for a job/school
☐ 9. Express gratitude for a great class

My School's Tutoring Center
Address:
Phone:
E-mail:
Day(s):
Time:
Tutor's Name and E-mail:

My Study Buddies Contact Information

Classmate:
Phone #:
E-mail:

Classmate:
Phone #:
E-mail:

Classmate:
Phone #:
E-mail:

The Superhighway of Academic Success

The Academic Facts Move from a Blackboard, to a Notebook, to a Homework Assignment, Through Your Powerful Brain, and to a Test

Learn to Listen and Listen to Learn

ACANDY In-Class Active Listening Skills

1. Pre-read the lecture topic. ✔

2. Clear your mind of all distractions (thoughts, feelings: worry, anxiety, and fear). ✔

3. Focus. Follow the speaker's line of argument. ✔

4. Selectively listen for the key facts, phrases, and words. ✔

5. What does the speaker focus on? Concepts? Formulas? ✔

6. As questions arise, write them down in the margins of your notebook. ✔

7. Ask your teacher for clarification. ✔

8. Do not leave class feeling lost, confused, or hopeless. ✔

Plan Your Work and Work Your Plan

ACANDY In-Class Note Taking Skills

1. Take organized notes: Write down the main ideas and supporting details. ✔

2. To write quickly, use abbreviations and shorthand symbols. ✔

3. Bring extra pens and pencils. ✔

4. Write the homework assignment down in a SMARTGRADES Academic Assignment Planner (not in your head) and double check it for accuracy. ✔

Failing to Prepare Is Preparing to Fail

ACANDY After-Class Test Review Notes to Ace Your Test

1. Choose a study area that is free of external and social distractions: _desk_ ✔

2. Eat a **Power Study Snack** to stay energized and focused (see list): _cookies_ ✔

3. **Manage your time.** ✔
Estimate Time (Fantasy):   Start Time: Finish Time: **Actual Time (Reality):**

4. After every class, read your class notes and underline/highlight the <u>main ideas</u> and <u>supporting details.</u> ✔

5. **Condensation** (Distillation): Outline/summarize your class notes into **Test Review Notes.** ✔

6. Do the facts need further clarification (see another textbook, tutoring center, or teacher)? ✔

7. Visualize the test question. Convert the facts into a test question: Define Terms? Compare? Contrast? Cause and Effect? Pros and Cons? List? Prove? Discuss? Outline? Agree or Disagree? ✔

8. Use **Association Cues** to memorize facts for **Instant and Total Recall.** Attach an unknown fact to a known fact stored in your memory. Use very personal memories for higher rates of retention. ✔

Acrostic Cue: Use a sentence to condense the key facts. For example, to remember the order of G-clef notes on sheet music, (E, G, B, D, F,) use the classic acrostic: Every Good Boy Deserves Fun.

Rhyme Cue: Use rhymes to link the key facts together. For example, the classic, "I before E, except after C."

Music Cue: Make up a song or poem with the information in it. Sing the song or recite the poem several times.

Chaining Cue: Create a story where each word or idea you have to remember cues the next idea you need to recall. Use your imagination. If you had to remember the name, Shirley Temple, you could rhyme Shirley with curly and remember that she had curly hair around her temples.

Funny Cue: Write a joke that contains the key facts. The funniest, most outlandish, and the strangest concoction of memory cues makes memorizing easy.

9. Two weeks before the test, **Self-Test** for strengths and weaknesses (change weak cues). ✔

10. The day of the test, review your study notes to refresh your memory. Ace the Test. ✔

Make the Grade and Achieve the Dream

My Class Notes Date:

Topic:

Write down the **Main Idea** and the **supporting Details, Examples,** or **Arguments**:

My Class Notes Continued . . .

Part I: My Test Review Notes to Ace the Exam

1. Right after class, read your class notes, and condense them into **Test Review Notes**. ✔
2. Choose a study area that is free of external and social distractions: _____ ✔
3. Eat a **Power Study Snack** to stay energized and focused (see list): _____ ✔
4. Manage your time. ✔
      Estimate Time (Fantasy):   Start Time: Finish Time: **Actual Time (Reality):**
5. Do the facts need further clarification (see textbook, tutoring center, or teacher)? ✔
6. To ace your test, use **Association Cues** to memorize the facts for **Instant and Total Recall**. ✔

Fact 1: Memory Cue 1 (use a pencil to change or refine cues)

Part II: My Test Review Notes to Ace the Exam

7. **Visualize** the test questions. **Convert** the facts into test questions: Who? Why? Where? What? ✔

8. **Self-Test** for strengths and weaknesses. Change the weak memory cues. ✔

9. To ace your test: Review, Repetition, Retention, Recognition, and Instant and Total Recall. ✔

Fact 1: Test Question 1

My Class Notes Date:

Topic:

Write down the **Main Idea** and the **supporting Details, Examples,** or **Arguments**:

My Class Notes Continued . . .

My Class Notes Continued . . .

Part I: My Test Review Notes to Ace the Exam

1. Right after class, read your class notes, and condense them into **Test Review Notes.** ✔
2. Choose a study area that is free of external and social distractions: _____ ✔
3. Eat a **Power Study Snack** to stay energized and focused (see list): _____ ✔
4. Manage your time. ✔
       Estimate Time (Fantasy):   Start Time: Finish Time: **Actual Time (Reality):**
5. Do the facts need further clarification (see textbook, tutoring center, or teacher)? ✔
6. To ace your test, use **Association Cues** to memorize the facts for **Instant and Total Recall.** ✔

Fact 1: Memory Cue 1 (use a pencil to change or refine cues)

Part II: My Test Review Notes to Ace the Exam

7. **Visualize** the test questions. **Convert** the facts into test questions: Who? Why? Where? What? ✔

8. **Self-Test** for strengths and weaknesses. Change the weak memory cues. ✔

9. To ace your test: Review, Repetition, Retention, Recognition, and Instant and Total Recall. ✔

Fact 1: Test Question 1

My Class Notes   Date:

Topic:

Write down the **Main Idea** and the **supporting Details**, **Examples**, or **Arguments**:

My Class Notes Continued . . .

Part I: My Test Review Notes to Ace the Exam

1. Right after class, read your class notes, and condense them into **Test Review Notes.** ✔
2. Choose a study area that is free of external and social distractions: _____ ✔
3. Eat a **Power Study Snack** to stay energized and focused (see list): _____ ✔
4. Manage your time. ✔
   Estimate Time (Fantasy):   Start Time: Finish Time: **Actual Time (Reality):**
5. Do the facts need further clarification (see textbook, tutoring center, or teacher)? ✔
6. To ace your test, use **Association Cues** to memorize the facts for **Instant and Total Recall.** ✔

Fact 1: Memory Cue 1 (use a pencil to change or refine cues)

Part II: My Test Review Notes to Ace the Exam

7. **Visualize** the test questions. **Convert** the facts into test questions: Who? Why? Where? What? ✔

8. **Self-Test** for strengths and weaknesses. Change the weak memory cues. ✔

9. To ace your test: Review, Repetition, Retention, Recognition, and Instant and Total Recall. ✔

Fact 1: Test Question 1

My Class Notes Date:

Topic:

Write down the **Main Idea** and the **supporting Details, Examples,** or **Arguments**:

My Class Notes Continued . . .

Part I: My Test Review Notes to Ace the Exam

1. Right after class, read your class notes, and condense them into **Test Review Notes.** ✔
2. Choose a study area that is free of external and social distractions: _____ ✔
3. Eat a **Power Study Snack** to stay energized and focused (see list): _____ ✔
4. Manage your time. ✔
      Estimate Time (Fantasy):   Start Time: Finish Time: **Actual Time (Reality):**
5. Do the facts need further clarification (see textbook, tutoring center, or teacher)? ✔
6. To ace your test, use **Association Cues** to memorize the facts for **Instant and Total Recall.** ✔

Fact 1: Memory Cue 1 (use a pencil to change or refine cues)

Part II: My Test Review Notes to Ace the Exam

7. **Visualize** the test questions. **Convert** the facts into test questions: Who? Why? Where? What? ✔

8. **Self-Test** for strengths and weaknesses. Change the weak memory cues. ✔

9. To ace your test: Review, Repetition, Retention, Recognition, and Instant and Total Recall. ✔

Fact 1: Test Question 1

My Class Notes   Date:

Topic:

Write down the **Main Idea** and the **supporting Details, Examples,** or **Arguments:**

My Class Notes Continued . . .

Part I: My Test Review Notes to Ace the Exam

1. Right after class, read your class notes, and condense them into **Test Review Notes.** ✔
2. Choose a study area that is free of external and social distractions: _____ ✔
3. Eat a **Power Study Snack** to stay energized and focused (see list): _____ ✔
4. Manage your time. ✔
      Estimate Time (Fantasy):   Start Time: Finish Time: **Actual Time (Reality):**
5. Do the facts need further clarification (see textbook, tutoring center, or teacher)? ✔
6. To ace your test, use **Association Cues** to memorize the facts for **Instant and Total Recall.** ✔

Fact 1: Memory Cue 1 (use a pencil to change or refine cues)

Part II: My Test Review Notes to Ace the Exam

7. **Visualize** the test questions. **Convert** the facts into test questions: Who? Why? Where? What? ✔

8. **Self-Test** for strengths and weaknesses. Change the weak memory cues. ✔

9. To ace your test: Review, Repetition, Retention, Recognition, and Instant and Total Recall. ✔

Fact 1: Test Question 1

My Class Notes Date:

Topic:

Write down the **Main Idea** and the **supporting** Details, Examples, or Arguments:

My Class Notes Continued . . .

Part I: My Test Review Notes to Ace the Exam

1. Right after class, read your class notes, and condense them into **Test Review Notes.** ✔
2. Choose a study area that is free of external and social distractions: _____ ✔
3. Eat a **Power Study Snack** to stay energized and focused (see list): _____ ✔
4. Manage your time. ✔
    Estimate Time (Fantasy):   Start Time: Finish Time: **Actual Time (Reality):**
5. Do the facts need further clarification (see textbook, tutoring center, or teacher)? ✔
6. To ace your test, use **Association Cues** to memorize the facts for **Instant and Total Recall.** ✔

Fact 1: Memory Cue 1 (use a pencil to change or refine cues)

Part II: My Test Review Notes to Ace the Exam

7. **Visualize** the test questions. **Convert** the facts into test questions: Who? Why? Where? What? ✔

8. **Self-Test** for strengths and weaknesses. Change the weak memory cues. ✔

9. To ace your test: Review, Repetition, Retention, Recognition, and Instant and Total Recall. ✔

Fact 1: Test Question 1

My Class Notes　　　　　　　　　　　　　　　　　　　　　　　　Date:

Topic:

Write down the **Main Idea** and the **supporting Details, Examples,** or **Arguments**:

My Class Notes Continued . . .

Part I: My Test Review Notes to Ace the Exam

1. Right after class, read your class notes, and condense them into **Test Review Notes**. ✔
2. Choose a study area that is free of external and social distractions: _____ ✔
3. Eat a **Power Study Snack** to stay energized and focused (see list): _____ ✔
4. Manage your time. ✔
      Estimate Time (Fantasy):   Start Time: Finish Time: **Actual Time (Reality):**
5. Do the facts need further clarification (see textbook, tutoring center, or teacher)? ✔
6. To ace your test, use **Association Cues** to memorize the facts for **Instant and Total Recall**. ✔

Fact 1: Memory Cue 1 (use a pencil to change or refine cues)

Part II: My Test Review Notes to Ace the Exam

7. **Visualize** the test questions. **Convert** the facts into test questions: Who? Why? Where? What? ✔

8. **Self-Test** for strengths and weaknesses. Change the weak memory cues. ✔

9. To ace your test: Review, Repetition, Retention, Recognition, and Instant and Total Recall. ✔

Fact 1: Test Question 1

My Class Notes   Date:

Topic:

Write down the **Main Idea** and the **supporting** **Details**, **Examples**, or **Arguments**:

My Class Notes Continued . . .

Part I: My Test Review Notes to Ace the Exam

1. Right after class, read your class notes, and condense them into **Test Review Notes.** ✔
2. Choose a study area that is free of external and social distractions: _____ ✔
3. Eat a **Power Study Snack** to stay energized and focused (see list): _____ ✔
4. Manage your time. ✔
       Estimate Time (Fantasy):   Start Time: Finish Time: **Actual Time (Reality):**
5. Do the facts need further clarification (see textbook, tutoring center, or teacher)? ✔
6. To ace your test, use **Association Cues** to memorize the facts for **Instant and Total Recall.** ✔

Fact 1: Memory Cue 1 (use a pencil to change or refine cues)

Part II: My Test Review Notes to Ace the Exam

7. **Visualize** the test questions. **Convert** the facts into test questions: Who? Why? Where? What? ✔

8. **Self-Test** for strengths and weaknesses. Change the weak memory cues. ✔

9. To ace your test: Review, Repetition, Retention, Recognition, and Instant and Total Recall. ✔

Fact 1: Test Question 1

My Class Notes   Date:

Topic:

Write down the **Main Idea** and the **supporting Details**, **Examples**, or **Arguments**:

_____
_____
_____
_____
_____
_____
_____
_____
_____
_____
_____
_____
_____
_____
_____
_____
_____
_____
_____
_____
_____
_____
_____
_____
_____
_____
_____
_____
_____
_____
_____
_____
_____
_____
_____
_____

My Class Notes   Date:

Topic:

_____

My Class Notes Continued . . .

Part I: My Test Review Notes to Ace the Exam

1. Right after class, read your class notes, and condense them into **Test Review Notes.** ✔
2. Choose a study area that is free of external and social distractions: _____ ✔
3. Eat a **Power Study Snack** to stay energized and focused (see list): _____ ✔
4. Manage your time. ✔
   Estimate Time (Fantasy):   Start Time: Finish Time: **Actual Time (Reality):**
5. Do the facts need further clarification (see textbook, tutoring center, or teacher)? ✔
6. To ace your test, use **Association Cues** to memorize the facts for **Instant and Total Recall.** ✔

Fact 1: Memory Cue 1 (use a pencil to change or refine cues)

Part II: My Test Review Notes to Ace the Exam

7. **Visualize** the test questions. **Convert** the facts into test questions: Who? Why? Where? What? ✔

8. **Self-Test** for strengths and weaknesses. Change the weak memory cues. ✔

9. To ace your test: Review, Repetition, Retention, Recognition, and Instant and Total Recall. ✔

Fact 1: Test Question 1

My Class Notes Date:

Topic:

Write down the **Main Idea** and the **supporting** Details, Examples, or Arguments:

My Class Notes Continued . . .

Part I: My Test Review Notes to Ace the Exam

1. Right after class, read your class notes, and condense them into **Test Review Notes**. ✔
2. Choose a study area that is free of external and social distractions: _____ ✔
3. Eat a **Power Study Snack** to stay energized and focused (see list): _____ ✔
4. Manage your time. ✔
      Estimate Time (Fantasy):   Start Time: Finish Time: **Actual Time (Reality):**
5. Do the facts need further clarification (see textbook, tutoring center, or teacher)? ✔
6. To ace your test, use **Association Cues** to memorize the facts for **Instant and Total Recall**. ✔

Fact 1: Memory Cue 1 (use a pencil to change or refine cues)

Part II: My Test Review Notes to Ace the Exam

7. **Visualize** the test questions. **Convert** the facts into test questions: Who? Why? Where? What? ✔

8. **Self-Test** for strengths and weaknesses. Change the weak memory cues. ✔

9. To ace your test: Review, Repetition, Retention, Recognition, and Instant and Total Recall. ✔

Fact 1: Test Question 1

My Class Notes Date:

Topic:

Write down the **Main Idea** and the **supporting Details, Examples,** or **Arguments**:

My Class Notes Continued . . .

Part I: My Test Review Notes to Ace the Exam

1. Right after class, read your class notes, and condense them into **Test Review Notes.** ✔
2. Choose a study area that is free of external and social distractions: _____ ✔
3. Eat a **Power Study Snack** to stay energized and focused (see list): _____ ✔
4. Manage your time. ✔
      Estimate Time (Fantasy):   Start Time: Finish Time: **Actual Time (Reality):**
5. Do the facts need further clarification (see textbook, tutoring center, or teacher)? ✔
6. To ace your test, use **Association Cues** to memorize the facts for **Instant and Total Recall.** ✔

Fact 1: Memory Cue 1 (use a pencil to change or refine cues)

Part II: My Test Review Notes to Ace the Exam

7. **Visualize** the test questions. **Convert** the facts into test questions: Who? Why? Where? What? ✔

8. **Self-Test** for strengths and weaknesses. Change the weak memory cues. ✔

9. To ace your test: Review, Repetition, Retention, Recognition, and Instant and Total Recall. ✔

Fact 1: Test Question 1

My Class Notes Date:

Topic:

Write down the **Main Idea** and the **supporting Details, Examples,** or **Arguments:**

My Class Notes Continued . . .

Part I: My Test Review Notes to Ace the Exam

1. Right after class, read your class notes, and condense them into **Test Review Notes**. ✔
2. Choose a study area that is free of external and social distractions: _____ ✔
3. Eat a **Power Study Snack** to stay energized and focused (see list): _____ ✔
4. Manage your time. ✔
      Estimate Time (Fantasy):   Start Time: Finish Time: **Actual Time (Reality):**
5. Do the facts need further clarification (see textbook, tutoring center, or teacher)? ✔
6. To ace your test, use **Association Cues** to memorize the facts for **Instant and Total Recall**. ✔

Fact 1: Memory Cue 1 (use a pencil to change or refine cues)

Part II: My Test Review Notes to Ace the Exam

7. **Visualize** the test questions. **Convert** the facts into test questions: Who? Why? Where? What? ✔

8. **Self-Test** for strengths and weaknesses. Change the weak memory cues. ✔

9. To ace your test: Review, Repetition, Retention, Recognition, and Instant and Total Recall. ✔

Fact 1: Test Question 1

My Class Notes Date:

Topic:

Write down the **Main Idea** and the **supporting Details, Examples,** or **Arguments**:

My Class Notes Continued . . .

Part I: My Test Review Notes to Ace the Exam

1. Right after class, read your class notes, and condense them into **Test Review Notes**. ✔
2. Choose a study area that is free of external and social distractions: _____ ✔
3. Eat a **Power Study Snack** to stay energized and focused (see list): _____ ✔
4. Manage your time. ✔
    Estimate Time (Fantasy):   Start Time: Finish Time: **Actual Time (Reality):**
5. Do the facts need further clarification (see textbook, tutoring center, or teacher)? ✔
6. To ace your test, use **Association Cues** to memorize the facts for **Instant and Total Recall**. ✔

Fact 1: Memory Cue 1 (use a pencil to change or refine cues)

Part II: My Test Review Notes to Ace the Exam

7. **Visualize** the test questions. **Convert** the facts into test questions: Who? Why? Where? What? ✔

8. **Self-Test** for strengths and weaknesses. Change the weak memory cues. ✔

9. To ace your test: Review, Repetition, Retention, Recognition, and Instant and Total Recall. ✔

Fact 1: Test Question 1

My Class Notes   Date:

Topic:

Write down the **Main Idea** and the **supporting** <u>Details</u>, <u>Examples</u>, or <u>Arguments</u>:
_____
_____
_____
_____
_____
_____
_____
_____
_____
_____
_____
_____
_____
_____
_____
_____
_____
_____
_____
_____
_____
_____
_____
_____
_____
_____
_____
_____
_____
_____
_____
_____
_____
_____
_____

My Class Notes   Date:

Topic:
_____
_____

My Class Notes Continued . . .

Part I: My Test Review Notes to Ace the Exam

1. Right after class, read your class notes, and condense them into **Test Review Notes**. ✔
2. Choose a study area that is free of external and social distractions: _____ ✔
3. Eat a **Power Study Snack** to stay energized and focused (see list): _____ ✔
4. Manage your time. ✔
      Estimate Time (Fantasy):   Start Time: Finish Time: **Actual Time (Reality):**
5. Do the facts need further clarification (see textbook, tutoring center, or teacher)? ✔
6. To ace your test, use **Association Cues** to memorize the facts for **Instant and Total Recall**. ✔

Fact 1: Memory Cue 1 (use a pencil to change or refine cues)

Part II: My Test Review Notes to Ace the Exam

7. **Visualize** the test questions. **Convert** the facts into test questions: Who? Why? Where? What? ✔

8. **Self-Test** for strengths and weaknesses. Change the weak memory cues. ✔

9. To ace your test: Review, Repetition, Retention, Recognition, and Instant and Total Recall. ✔

Fact 1: Test Question 1

My Class Notes Date:

Topic:

Write down the **Main Idea** and the **supporting Details**, **Examples**, or **Arguments**:

My Class Notes Continued . . .

Part I: My Test Review Notes to Ace the Exam

1. Right after class, read your class notes, and condense them into **Test Review Notes**. ✔
2. Choose a study area that is free of external and social distractions: _____ ✔
3. Eat a **Power Study Snack** to stay energized and focused (see list): _____ ✔
4. Manage your time. ✔
      Estimate Time (Fantasy):   Start Time: Finish Time: **Actual Time (Reality):**
5. Do the facts need further clarification (see textbook, tutoring center, or teacher)? ✔
6. To ace your test, use **Association Cues** to memorize the facts for **Instant and Total Recall**. ✔

Fact 1: Memory Cue 1 (use a pencil to change or refine cues)

Part II: My Test Review Notes to Ace the Exam

7. **Visualize** the test questions. **Convert** the facts into test questions: Who? Why? Where? What? ✔

8. **Self-Test** for strengths and weaknesses. Change the weak memory cues. ✔

9. To ace your test: Review, Repetition, Retention, Recognition, and Instant and Total Recall. ✔

Fact 1: Test Question 1

My Class Notes   Date:

Topic:

Write down the **Main Idea** and the **supporting Details**, **Examples**, or **Arguments**:

_____
_____
_____
_____
_____
_____
_____
_____
_____
_____
_____
_____
_____
_____
_____
_____
_____
_____
_____
_____
_____
_____
_____
_____
_____
_____
_____
_____
_____
_____
_____
_____

My Class Notes   Date:

Topic:

_____

My Class Notes Continued . . .

Part I: My Test Review Notes to Ace the Exam

1. Right after class, read your class notes, and condense them into **Test Review Notes.** ✔
2. Choose a study area that is free of external and social distractions: _____ ✔
3. Eat a **Power Study Snack** to stay energized and focused (see list): _____ ✔
4. Manage your time. ✔
   Estimate Time (Fantasy):   Start Time: Finish Time: **Actual Time (Reality):**
5. Do the facts need further clarification (see textbook, tutoring center, or teacher)? ✔
6. To ace your test, use **Association Cues** to memorize the facts for **Instant and Total Recall.** ✔

Fact 1: Memory Cue 1 (use a pencil to change or refine cues)

Part II: My Test Review Notes to Ace the Exam

7. **Visualize** the test questions. **Convert** the facts into test questions: Who? Why? Where? What? ✔

8. **Self-Test** for strengths and weaknesses. Change the weak memory cues. ✔

9. To ace your test: Review, Repetition, Retention, Recognition, and Instant and Total Recall. ✔

Fact 1: Test Question 1

My Class Notes Date:

Topic:

Write down the **Main Idea** and the **supporting Details**, **Examples**, or **Arguments**:

My Class Notes Continued . . .

Part I: My Test Review Notes to Ace the Exam

1. Right after class, read your class notes, and condense them into **Test Review Notes**. ✔
2. Choose a study area that is free of external and social distractions: _____ ✔
3. Eat a **Power Study Snack** to stay energized and focused (see list): _____ ✔
4. Manage your time. ✔
    Estimate Time (Fantasy):   Start Time: Finish Time: **Actual Time (Reality):**
5. Do the facts need further clarification (see textbook, tutoring center, or teacher)? ✔
6. To ace your test, use **Association Cues** to memorize the facts for **Instant and Total Recall**. ✔

Fact 1: Memory Cue 1 (use a pencil to change or refine cues)

Part II: My Test Review Notes to Ace the Exam

7. **Visualize** the test questions. **Convert** the facts into test questions: Who? Why? Where? What? ✔

8. **Self-Test** for strengths and weaknesses. Change the weak memory cues. ✔

9. To ace your test: Review, Repetition, Retention, Recognition, and Instant and Total Recall. ✔

Fact 1: Test Question 1

My Class Notes   Date:

Topic:

Write down the **Main Idea** and the **supporting** <u>Details</u>, <u>Examples</u>, or <u>Arguments</u>:

My Class Notes Continued . . .

Part I: My Test Review Notes to Ace the Exam

1. Right after class, read your class notes, and condense them into **Test Review Notes**. ✔
2. Choose a study area that is free of external and social distractions: _____ ✔
3. Eat a **Power Study Snack** to stay energized and focused (see list): _____ ✔
4. Manage your time. ✔
    Estimate Time (Fantasy):   Start Time: Finish Time: **Actual Time (Reality):**
5. Do the facts need further clarification (see textbook, tutoring center, or teacher)? ✔
6. To ace your test, use **Association Cues** to memorize the facts for **Instant and Total Recall**. ✔

Fact 1: Memory Cue 1 (use a pencil to change or refine cues)

Part II: My Test Review Notes to Ace the Exam

7. **Visualize** the test questions. **Convert** the facts into test questions: Who? Why? Where? What? ✔

8. **Self-Test** for strengths and weaknesses. Change the weak memory cues. ✔

9. To ace your test: Review, Repetition, Retention, Recognition, and Instant and Total Recall. ✔

Fact 1: Test Question 1

My Class Notes　　　　　　　　　　　　　　　　　　　　　　　　　　Date:

Topic:

Write down the **Main Idea** and the **supporting Details**, **Examples**, or **Arguments**:

My Class Notes Continued . . .

Part I: My Test Review Notes to Ace the Exam

1. Right after class, read your class notes, and condense them into **Test Review Notes**. ✔
2. Choose a study area that is free of external and social distractions: _____ ✔
3. Eat a **Power Study Snack** to stay energized and focused (see list): _____ ✔
4. Manage your time. ✔
      Estimate Time (Fantasy):   Start Time: Finish Time: **Actual Time (Reality):**
5. Do the facts need further clarification (see textbook, tutoring center, or teacher)? ✔
6. To ace your test, use **Association Cues** to memorize the facts for **Instant and Total Recall**. ✔

Fact 1: Memory Cue 1 (use a pencil to change or refine cues)

Part II: My Test Review Notes to Ace the Exam

7. **Visualize** the test questions. **Convert** the facts into test questions: Who? Why? Where? What? ✔

8. **Self-Test** for strengths and weaknesses. Change the weak memory cues. ✔

9. To ace your test: Review, Repetition, Retention, Recognition, and Instant and Total Recall. ✔

Fact 1: Test Question 1

My Class Notes   Date:

Topic:

Write down the **Main Idea** and the **supporting Details, Examples,** or **Arguments**:

_____
_____
_____
_____
_____
_____
_____
_____
_____
_____
_____
_____
_____
_____
_____
_____
_____
_____
_____
_____
_____
_____
_____
_____
_____
_____
_____
_____
_____
_____
_____

My Class Notes   Date:

Topic:

_____

My Class Notes Continued . . .

Part I: My Test Review Notes to Ace the Exam

1. Right after class, read your class notes, and condense them into **Test Review Notes**. ✔
2. Choose a study area that is free of external and social distractions: _____ ✔
3. Eat a **Power Study Snack** to stay energized and focused (see list): _____ ✔
4. Manage your time. ✔
    Estimate Time (Fantasy):   Start Time: Finish Time: **Actual Time (Reality):**
5. Do the facts need further clarification (see textbook, tutoring center, or teacher)? ✔
6. To ace your test, use **Association Cues** to memorize the facts for **Instant and Total Recall**. ✔

Fact 1: Memory Cue 1 (use a pencil to change or refine cues)

Part II: My Test Review Notes to Ace the Exam

7. **Visualize** the test questions. **Convert** the facts into test questions: Who? Why? Where? What? ✔

8. **Self-Test** for strengths and weaknesses. Change the weak memory cues. ✔

9. To ace your test: Review, Repetition, Retention, Recognition, and Instant and Total Recall. ✔

Fact 1: Test Question 1

My Class Notes Date:

Topic:

Write down the **Main Idea** and the **supporting Details**, **Examples**, or **Arguments**:

My Class Notes Date:

Topic:

My Class Notes Continued . . .

Part I: My Test Review Notes to Ace the Exam

1. Right after class, read your class notes, and condense them into **Test Review Notes**. ✔
2. Choose a study area that is free of external and social distractions: _____ ✔
3. Eat a **Power Study Snack** to stay energized and focused (see list): _____ ✔
4. Manage your time. ✔
    Estimate Time (Fantasy):   Start Time: Finish Time: **Actual Time (Reality):**
5. Do the facts need further clarification (see textbook, tutoring center, or teacher)? ✔
6. To ace your test, use **Association Cues** to memorize the facts for **Instant and Total Recall**. ✔

Fact 1: Memory Cue 1 (use a pencil to change or refine cues)

Part II: My Test Review Notes to Ace the Exam

7. **Visualize** the test questions. **Convert** the facts into test questions: Who? Why? Where? What? ✔

8. **Self-Test** for strengths and weaknesses. Change the weak memory cues. ✔

9. To ace your test: Review, Repetition, Retention, Recognition, and Instant and Total Recall. ✔

Fact 1: Test Question 1

My Class Notes Date:

Topic:

Write down the **Main Idea** and the **supporting** Details, Examples, or Arguments:

My Class Notes Continued . . .

Part I: My Test Review Notes to Ace the Exam

1. Right after class, read your class notes, and condense them into **Test Review Notes.** ✔
2. Choose a study area that is free of external and social distractions: _____ ✔
3. Eat a **Power Study Snack** to stay energized and focused (see list): _____ ✔
4. Manage your time. ✔
    Estimate Time (Fantasy):   Start Time: Finish Time: **Actual Time (Reality):**
5. Do the facts need further clarification (see textbook, tutoring center, or teacher)? ✔
6. To ace your test, use **Association Cues** to memorize the facts for **Instant and Total Recall.** ✔

Fact 1: Memory Cue 1 (use a pencil to change or refine cues)

Part II: My Test Review Notes to Ace the Exam

7. **Visualize** the test questions. **Convert** the facts into test questions: Who? Why? Where? What? ✔

8. **Self-Test** for strengths and weaknesses. Change the weak memory cues. ✔

9. To ace your test: Review, Repetition, Retention, Recognition, and Instant and Total Recall. ✔

Fact 1: Test Question 1

My Class Notes Date:

Topic:

Write down the **Main Idea** and the **supporting Details**, **Examples**, or **Arguments**:

My Class Notes Date:

Topic:

My Class Notes Continued . . .

Part I: My Test Review Notes to Ace the Exam

1. Right after class, read your class notes, and condense them into **Test Review Notes.** ✔
2. Choose a study area that is free of external and social distractions: _____ ✔
3. Eat a **Power Study Snack** to stay energized and focused (see list): _____ ✔
4. Manage your time. ✔
      Estimate Time (Fantasy):   Start Time: Finish Time: **Actual Time (Reality):**
5. Do the facts need further clarification (see textbook, tutoring center, or teacher)? ✔
6. To ace your test, use **Association Cues** to memorize the facts for **Instant and Total Recall.** ✔

Fact 1: Memory Cue 1 (use a pencil to change or refine cues)

Part II: My Test Review Notes to Ace the Exam

7. **Visualize** the test questions. **Convert** the facts into test questions: Who? Why? Where? What? ✔

8. **Self-Test** for strengths and weaknesses. Change the weak memory cues. ✔

9. To ace your test: Review, Repetition, Retention, Recognition, and Instant and Total Recall. ✔

Fact 1: Test Question 1

My Class Notes　　　　　　　　　　　　　　　　　　　　　　　　Date:

Topic:

Write down the **Main Idea** and the **supporting Details**, **Examples**, or **Arguments**:

My Class Notes Continued . . .

Part I: My Test Review Notes to Ace the Exam

1. Right after class, read your class notes, and condense them into **Test Review Notes**. ✔
2. Choose a study area that is free of external and social distractions: _____ ✔
3. Eat a **Power Study Snack** to stay energized and focused (see list): _____ ✔
4. Manage your time. ✔

    Estimate Time (Fantasy):   Start Time: Finish Time: **Actual Time (Reality):**

5. Do the facts need further clarification (see textbook, tutoring center, or teacher)? ✔
6. To ace your test, use **Association Cues** to memorize the facts for **Instant and Total Recall**. ✔

Fact 1: Memory Cue 1 (use a pencil to change or refine cues)

Part II: My Test Review Notes to Ace the Exam

7. **Visualize** the test questions. **Convert** the facts into test questions: Who? Why? Where? What? ✔

8. **Self-Test** for strengths and weaknesses. Change the weak memory cues. ✔

9. To ace your test: Review, Repetition, Retention, Recognition, and Instant and Total Recall. ✔

Fact 1: Test Question 1

My Class Notes　　　　　　　　　　　　　　　　　　　　　　　　Date:

Topic:

Write down the **Main Idea** and the **supporting Details**, **Examples**, or **Arguments**:

My Class Notes Continued . . .

Part I: My Test Review Notes to Ace the Exam

1. Right after class, read your class notes, and condense them into **Test Review Notes.** ✔
2. Choose a study area that is free of external and social distractions: _____ ✔
3. Eat a **Power Study Snack** to stay energized and focused (see list): _____ ✔
4. Manage your time. ✔
      Estimate Time (Fantasy):   Start Time: Finish Time: **Actual Time (Reality):**
5. Do the facts need further clarification (see textbook, tutoring center, or teacher)? ✔
6. To ace your test, use **Association Cues** to memorize the facts for **Instant and Total Recall.** ✔

Fact 1: Memory Cue 1 (use a pencil to change or refine cues)

Part II: My Test Review Notes to Ace the Exam

7. **Visualize** the test questions. **Convert** the facts into test questions: Who? Why? Where? What? ✔

8. **Self-Test** for strengths and weaknesses. Change the weak memory cues. ✔

9. To ace your test: Review, Repetition, Retention, Recognition, and Instant and Total Recall. ✔

Fact 1: Test Question 1

My Class Notes　　　　　　　　　　　　　　　　　　　　　　　　　　Date:

Topic:

Write down the **Main Idea** and the **supporting Details**, **Examples**, or **Arguments**:

My Class Notes Continued . . .

Part I: My Test Review Notes to Ace the Exam

1. Right after class, read your class notes, and condense them into **Test Review Notes.** ✔
2. Choose a study area that is free of external and social distractions: _____ ✔
3. Eat a **Power Study Snack** to stay energized and focused (see list): _____ ✔
4. Manage your time. ✔
    Estimate Time (Fantasy):   Start Time: Finish Time: **Actual Time (Reality):**
5. Do the facts need further clarification (see textbook, tutoring center, or teacher)? ✔
6. To ace your test, use **Association Cues** to memorize the facts for **Instant and Total Recall.** ✔

Fact 1: Memory Cue 1 (use a pencil to change or refine cues)

Part II: My Test Review Notes to Ace the Exam

7. **Visualize** the test questions. **Convert** the facts into test questions: Who? Why? Where? What? ✔

8. **Self-Test** for strengths and weaknesses. Change the weak memory cues. ✔

9. To ace your test: Review, Repetition, Retention, Recognition, and Instant and Total Recall. ✔

Fact 1: Test Question 1

My Class Notes Date:

Topic:

Write down the **Main Idea** and the **supporting Details, Examples,** or **Arguments**:

My Class Notes Continued . . .

Part I: My Test Review Notes to Ace the Exam

1. Right after class, read your class notes, and condense them into **Test Review Notes**. ✔
2. Choose a study area that is free of external and social distractions: _____ ✔
3. Eat a **Power Study Snack** to stay energized and focused (see list): _____ ✔
4. Manage your time. ✔
      Estimate Time (Fantasy):   Start Time: Finish Time: **Actual Time (Reality):**
5. Do the facts need further clarification (see textbook, tutoring center, or teacher)? ✔
6. To ace your test, use **Association Cues** to memorize the facts for **Instant and Total Recall**. ✔

Fact 1: Memory Cue 1 (use a pencil to change or refine cues)

Part II: My Test Review Notes to Ace the Exam

7. **Visualize** the test questions. **Convert** the facts into test questions: Who? Why? Where? What? ✔

8. **Self-Test** for strengths and weaknesses. Change the weak memory cues. ✔

9. To ace your test: Review, Repetition, Retention, Recognition, and Instant and Total Recall. ✔

Fact 1: Test Question 1

My Class Notes   Date:

Topic:

Write down the **Main Idea** and the **supporting Details, Examples,** or **Arguments**:

_____
_____
_____
_____
_____
_____
_____
_____
_____
_____
_____
_____
_____
_____
_____
_____
_____
_____
_____
_____
_____
_____
_____
_____
_____
_____
_____
_____
_____

My Class Notes   Date:

Topic:

_____

My Class Notes Continued . . .

Part I: My Test Review Notes to Ace the Exam

1. Right after class, read your class notes, and condense them into **Test Review Notes**. ✔
2. Choose a study area that is free of external and social distractions: _____ ✔
3. Eat a **Power Study Snack** to stay energized and focused (see list): _____ ✔
4. Manage your time. ✔
    Estimate Time (Fantasy):   Start Time: Finish Time: **Actual Time (Reality):**
5. Do the facts need further clarification (see textbook, tutoring center, or teacher)? ✔
6. To ace your test, use **Association Cues** to memorize the facts for **Instant and Total Recall**. ✔

Fact 1: Memory Cue 1 (use a pencil to change or refine cues)

Part II: My Test Review Notes to Ace the Exam

7. **Visualize** the test questions. **Convert** the facts into test questions: Who? Why? Where? What? ✔

8. **Self-Test** for strengths and weaknesses. Change the weak memory cues. ✔

9. To ace your test: Review, Repetition, Retention, Recognition, and Instant and Total Recall. ✔

Fact 1: Test Question 1

My Class Notes Date:

Topic:

Write down the **Main Idea** and the **supporting Details**, **Examples**, or **Arguments**:

My Class Notes Continued . . .

Part I: My Test Review Notes to Ace the Exam

1. Right after class, read your class notes, and condense them into **Test Review Notes**. ✔
2. Choose a study area that is free of external and social distractions: _____ ✔
3. Eat a **Power Study Snack** to stay energized and focused (see list): _____ ✔
4. Manage your time. ✔
   Estimate Time (Fantasy):   Start Time: Finish Time: **Actual Time (Reality):**
5. Do the facts need further clarification (see textbook, tutoring center, or teacher)? ✔
6. To ace your test, use **Association Cues** to memorize the facts for **Instant and Total Recall**. ✔

Fact 1: Memory Cue 1 (use a pencil to change or refine cues)

Part II: My Test Review Notes to Ace the Exam

7. **Visualize** the test questions. **Convert** the facts into test questions: Who? Why? Where? What? ✔

8. **Self-Test** for strengths and weaknesses. Change the weak memory cues. ✔

9. To ace your test: Review, Repetition, Retention, Recognition, and Instant and Total Recall. ✔

Fact 1: Test Question 1

My Class Notes　　　　　　　　　　　　　　　　　　　　　　　　　　　　Date:

Topic:

Write down the **Main Idea** and the **supporting Details**, **Examples**, or **Arguments**:

My Class Notes Continued . . .

Part I: My Test Review Notes to Ace the Exam

1. Right after class, read your class notes, and condense them into **Test Review Notes.** ✔
2. Choose a study area that is free of external and social distractions: _____ ✔
3. Eat a **Power Study Snack** to stay energized and focused (see list): _____ ✔
4. Manage your time. ✔
      Estimate Time (Fantasy):   Start Time: Finish Time: **Actual Time (Reality):**
5. Do the facts need further clarification (see textbook, tutoring center, or teacher)? ✔
6. To ace your test, use **Association Cues** to memorize the facts for **Instant and Total Recall.** ✔

Fact 1: Memory Cue 1 (use a pencil to change or refine cues)

Part II: My Test Review Notes to Ace the Exam

7. **Visualize** the test questions. **Convert** the facts into test questions: Who? Why? Where? What? ✔

8. **Self-Test** for strengths and weaknesses. Change the weak memory cues. ✔

9. To ace your test: Review, Repetition, Retention, Recognition, and Instant and Total Recall. ✔

Fact 1: Test Question 1

My Class Notes Date:

Topic:

Write down the **Main Idea** and the **supporting Details**, **Examples**, or **Arguments**:

My Class Notes Continued . . .

Part I: My Test Review Notes to Ace the Exam

1. Right after class, read your class notes, and condense them into **Test Review Notes.** ✔
2. Choose a study area that is free of external and social distractions: _____ ✔
3. Eat a **Power Study Snack** to stay energized and focused (see list): _____ ✔
4. Manage your time. ✔
   Estimate Time (Fantasy):   Start Time: Finish Time: **Actual Time (Reality):**
5. Do the facts need further clarification (see textbook, tutoring center, or teacher)? ✔
6. To ace your test, use **Association Cues** to memorize the facts for **Instant and Total Recall.** ✔

Fact 1: Memory Cue 1 (use a pencil to change or refine cues)

Part II: My Test Review Notes to Ace the Exam

7. **Visualize** the test questions. **Convert** the facts into test questions: Who? Why? Where? What? ✔

8. **Self-Test** for strengths and weaknesses. Change the weak memory cues. ✔

9. To ace your test: Review, Repetition, Retention, Recognition, and Instant and Total Recall. ✔

Fact 1: Test Question 1

My Class Notes Date:

Topic:

Write down the **Main Idea** and the **supporting Details, Examples,** or **Arguments**:

My Class Notes Continued . . .

Part I: My Test Review Notes to Ace the Exam

1. Right after class, read your class notes, and condense them into **Test Review Notes.** ✔
2. Choose a study area that is free of external and social distractions: _____ ✔
3. Eat a **Power Study Snack** to stay energized and focused (see list): _____ ✔
4. Manage your time. ✔
      Estimate Time (Fantasy):   Start Time: Finish Time: **Actual Time (Reality):**
5. Do the facts need further clarification (see textbook, tutoring center, or teacher)? ✔
6. To ace your test, use **Association Cues** to memorize the facts for **Instant and Total Recall.** ✔

Fact 1: Memory Cue 1 (use a pencil to change or refine cues)

Part II: My Test Review Notes to Ace the Exam

7. **Visualize** the test questions. **Convert** the facts into test questions: Who? Why? Where? What? ✔

8. **Self-Test** for strengths and weaknesses. Change the weak memory cues. ✔

9. To ace your test: Review, Repetition, Retention, Recognition, and Instant and Total Recall. ✔

Fact 1: Test Question 1

My Class Notes Date:

Topic:

Write down the **Main Idea** and the **supporting Details, Examples,** or **Arguments**:

My Class Notes Continued . . .

Part I: My Test Review Notes to Ace the Exam

1. Right after class, read your class notes, and condense them into **Test Review Notes.** ✔
2. Choose a study area that is free of external and social distractions: _____ ✔
3. Eat a **Power Study Snack** to stay energized and focused (see list): _____ ✔
4. Manage your time. ✔
    Estimate Time (Fantasy):   Start Time: Finish Time: **Actual Time (Reality):**
5. Do the facts need further clarification (see textbook, tutoring center, or teacher)? ✔
6. To ace your test, use **Association Cues** to memorize the facts for **Instant and Total Recall.** ✔

Fact 1: Memory Cue 1 (use a pencil to change or refine cues)

Part II: My Test Review Notes to Ace the Exam

7. **Visualize** the test questions. **Convert** the facts into test questions: Who? Why? Where? What? ✔

8. **Self-Test** for strengths and weaknesses. Change the weak memory cues. ✔

9. To ace your test: Review, Repetition, Retention, Recognition, and Instant and Total Recall. ✔

Fact 1: Test Question 1

My Class Notes Date:

Topic:

Write down the **Main Idea** and the **supporting Details, Examples,** or **Arguments**:

My Class Notes Continued . . .

Part I: My Test Review Notes to Ace the Exam

1. Right after class, read your class notes, and condense them into **Test Review Notes.** ✔
2. Choose a study area that is free of external and social distractions: _____ ✔
3. Eat a **Power Study Snack** to stay energized and focused (see list): _____ ✔
4. Manage your time. ✔
      Estimate Time (Fantasy):   Start Time: Finish Time: **Actual Time (Reality):**
5. Do the facts need further clarification (see textbook, tutoring center, or teacher)? ✔
6. To ace your test, use **Association Cues** to memorize the facts for **Instant and Total Recall.** ✔

Fact 1: Memory Cue 1 (use a pencil to change or refine cues)

Part II: My Test Review Notes to Ace the Exam

7. **Visualize** the test questions. **Convert** the facts into test questions: Who? Why? Where? What? ✔

8. **Self-Test** for strengths and weaknesses. Change the weak memory cues. ✔

9. To ace your test: Review, Repetition, Retention, Recognition, and Instant and Total Recall. ✔

Fact 1: Test Question 1

My Class Notes Date:

Topic:

Write down the **Main Idea** and the **supporting Details**, **Examples**, or **Arguments**:

My Class Notes Continued . . .

Our Power Study Snack Suggestions

Choose One of Our Power Study Snacks or Create Your Own Energy Menu

1. **Nutritious Pizza** ✓
   Whole Wheat Pita, Mozzarella Cheese Slice, Tomato Slice, Basil Leaf, and Olive Oil
   Microwave 30 Seconds

2. **Humus and Veggies** ✓
   Carrots, Celery, Broccoli, Red Peppers . . .

3. **Bran Muffin** ✓
   Apple-Oat, Cranberry-Walnut, Banana-Pecan . . .

4. **Sports Bar with 10+ Grams of Protein** ✓
   Avoid High Amounts of Saturated Fat or Hydrogenated Vegetable Oils

5. A Small 3oz. Can of Tuna/Sardines with 4-6 Whole Grain Crackers ✓

6. One Container of Low Fat Yogurt Sprinkled with High Fiber Cereal and Fresh Fruit ✓

7. Whole-Grain Cereal with Fat Free or 1% Low Fat Milk and Fresh Fruit ✓

8. **Trail Mix: Your Favorite Nuts** ✓
   Peanuts, Almonds, Cashews, Pistachios with Raisins and Cranberries . . .

9. **Dried Fruit Mix: Your Favorite Fruits** ✓
   Apricots, Pineapple, Apple Chips, Banana Chips . . .

10. Vegetable Soup and a Slice of Whole Grain Bread ✓

11. Chocolate Smoothie: Chocolate Soy Milk, Peanut Butter, and Whey Protein ✓

12. Oatmeal-Raisin Cookie ✓

My Power Study Snacks

List Your Favorite Power Study Snacks to Stay Energized and Focused

1. _____

2. _____

3. _____

4. _____

5. _____

6. _____

7. _____

8. _____

9. _____

10. _____

Make the Grade and Achieve the Dream

#1 School Notebook for Academic Success

THE SWEET TASTE OF ACADEMIC SUCCESS
ACANDY PROCESSING TOOLS
NEW LEARNING TECHNOLOGY FOR
PEAK ACADEMIC PERFORMANCE

✔ How to Ace Every Test Every Time
✔ How to Memorize Facts for Instant and Total Recall
✔ How to Write a Grade A English Essay
✔ How to Write a Grade A Research Report
✔ How to Speed Read Your Textbook
✔ How to Proofread Your Paper to Perfection
✔ How to Ace a Multiple Choice Exam
✔ How to Ace an Essay Exam

SM@RTGRADES®
Good Grades Become Great Grades and Great Grades Become Grand Dreams
www.smartgrades.com

® All Rights Reserved.
The Great American Notebook Company
More School Smarts for the Same Smart Price
100 School Notebook Designs and Study Tools
www.aplusgrades.com

New Learning Technology for Peak Academic Performance

EVERY DAY AN EASY A

Elementary School Edition
High School Edition
College Edition

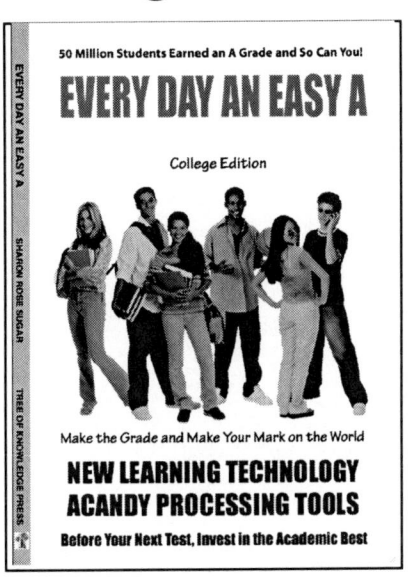

Tree of Knowledge Press
We Educate Children One Child at a Time
www.treeofknowledgepress.com

BEFORE YOUR NEXT TEST INVEST IN THE ACADEMIC BEST